MOVING PICTURES

MARTIN ZARROP

INDEPENDENT INNOVATIVE INTERNATIONAL

Published by Cinnamon Press
Meirion House
Tanygrisiau
Blaenau Ffestiniog
Gwynedd, LL41 3SU
www.cinnamonpress.com

The right of Martin Zarrop to be identified as author of this work has been asserted by him in accordance with the Copyright, Designs and Patent Act, 1988. Copyright © 2015 Martin Zarrop. ISBN:978-1-910836-33-0
British Library Cataloguing in Publication Data. A CIP record for this book can be obtained from the British Library.

Designed and typeset in Palatino by Cinnamon Press. Printed in Poland.

Original cover design by Adam Craig from original artwork Peerayot To-im © Dreamstime.com.

Cinnamon Press is represented in the UK by Inpress Ltd and in Wales by the Welsh Books Council.

Acknowledgments

Acknowledgments are due to the editors of the following publications in which versions of some of these poems have previously appeared: *Envoi, Poetry News, Prole, Never Bury Poetry, The Book of Love & Loss* (Belgrave Press, 2014), *Blame Montezuma!* (Happenstance, 2014) and *How Higher Education Feels* (Sense Publishers, 2016).

Album was Highly Commended in the 2012 Ledbury Poetry Competition.

Breaking the Rules (formerly *Planck)* was commended in the 2011 Stanza Poetry Competition ('Breaking the Rules')

Versions of *Dry Run, Maths Master I, Breaking the Rules, Moving Pictures, Hiroshima, Operation Paperclip, Ritual II* and *Album* have previously appeared in the author's pamphlet *No Theory of Everything* (Cinnamon Press, 2015), one of the winners of the 2014 Cinnamon Press Pamphlet Competition.

Trinity and *Hiroshima* quote freely from *The Making of the Atomic Bomb* by Richard Rhodes (Simon & Schuster, 1988).

Heartfelt thanks (once again) are due to Cross Border Poets, Chorlton Poetry Writers Study Group, Poem Shed, Ruthin Wheel Writers and, in particular, Richard Hughes, Robbie Burton, Vivien Finney and Alan Clemo for their encouragement and invaluable feedback.

Contents

for

Jean & Avril

and

Trevor & Paula

Moving Pictures

The Gift

i.m. Claudette

Your eyes were closed,
a small red flower on the pillow.
I didn't want to disturb you
with words. One kiss and I left.

The next day I busied myself
with all the expected stuff.
Every call was for me;
it didn't seem strange at the time.

People were friendlier than usual
but they didn't mention you.
Afterwards, pounding the hills,
I thought about black holes,

the problem of pain, and cried
about nothing in particular.
I felt something was wrong,
so I decided to write.

Act of Creation

He holds in his hands a square
of darkness, folds it with care,
folds it again until zero
curvature becomes fractal
mountain, tectonic plate.
He licks a finger, wets
the world into ocean shapes.

Now he is all thumbs,
fumbles with butterflies,
a lizard's slither over
wet sand, the lace of leaves
in sunlight. Laughter
wrinkles a human face,
the brain's glistening rills.

It has a mind to differ, defying
reason with each crease and twist
of its evolution and emerges,
as if by design, from the jungle,
a paper tiger, staring
through long grass
into the oncoming flames.

An Arsonist Grasps Olbers' Paradox

Behind cold bars
he stares through time
at the invisible, draws

lines in the sky to distant sparks
that refuse to fire the heavens.
In the stubborn dark, he sees

nothing is there
but the echoed hiss
of a violent birth.

The night light flickers,
dances with shadows
shifting into red.

Dry Run

Criccieth 2010

Beyond a chamber of clouds
the moon drags horses, kicking
onto a fractured beach.
Experts in anoraks, landscaped
like Gormley figures, notebooks in hand,
patiently record the next experiment.
Gulls trace their trajectories through mist
crying 'Higgs! Higgs! Higgs!'

The world is up and running
and a wave of probability collapses
onto an uncertain shore, where rocks
crack smiles like stranded whales.
Bladderwrack, blood-red and green,
dozes to the soft hiss of water.
It waits for the current's surge
as flies dart here and there
with their own theories
of everything.

Landers

Curiosity sailed with us to this place,
left us on a gale-torn shore,
held hope for new life.

No comradeship but our own,
we worked hard, bore the wind-rush
of mean air across an alien landscape.

We came to accept this home,
learned its strange ways,
called an uneasy truce.

Sometimes we look sunwards
into the past, knowing
we are all Martians now.

Bogeyman I

Once upon a time
there were no fairy tales
or deodorants, only
the smell of peeling wallpaper,
the sweat of Santa Claus
as someone locked the door,
assured me he didn't exist.
Happy ever after
is another story.

Train Set

Sewing machines clatter the attic space,
surround the birthday boy and his father
with adult laughter, the reek of tobacco.

Workshop windows, grimy with East End years,
filter winter light onto bare metal rails,
a circle of tin no bigger than a soup plate.

The red engine holds the key, racing
on its fixed orbit, to fall, stop, start,
repeat precisely its chosen path.

The grown-ups drift away to their worries:
Business is not so good, I tell you,
the ups and downs of the rag trade.

In his little world, clockwork rattles on
to the thump and hiss of pressured steam.

The Father-Thing

I saw eyes light up
as it checked each betting slip,
tailored its algorithms
to sweatshop speed

an amalgam of sewing machine,
calculator, seven-horse accumulator,
no template for a human
who demanded certainty.

All right, son? was the call sign
when I blipped on its radar
before the inevitable
short of a fiver

and the meter ticked on
as I oiled the mechanism.
It rarely malfunctioned,
only twice, I remember:

Are you getting your oats?
attempted connection
and, later, that *fuck*
was the mother of overloads.

I would talk to him now
but the language is lost,
a cipher of semaphore
and Masonic handshakes.

If there were thoughts,
they're gone with his laughter,
leaving the imprint,
no reboot possible.

Protection

This early, they haven't yet arrived.
Mick can open the workshop,
drink his tea, begin to mark up cloth
ready for cutting, a quiet time

waiting for the boys, their dirty jokes,
before the steam press hisses
to a crescendo of Singer machines,
the chaos of shouts and laughter

the boss joining in with his ball-breaking
and skilful fiddling in the back office,
anything to make a dollar, keep the work
coming in, week after grafting week.

It's still early but there's the weight
of a step on the wooden staircase.
For a moment, he doesn't recognize
the Saville Row suit, thick-set neck.

Now, he feels cold and a little sick,
naked in the face of authority:
Sam isn't in today, Mr Kray
but neither is my father's heart

as the customer turns to leave.
Tell him I'll be back, says Reggie
and smiles his business smile
for no one in particular.

Mr Green

My afternoon begins
with the sound of gunfire.
Desk lids fall in unison
as Mr Green strides in.

His face is impassive,
demanding obedience.
No boy moves a finger
as Mr Green fingers the window pole.
He studies the first three rows
of shorter pupils.

Mr Green remains impassive.
His voice *is* gunfire.
I don't remember
the subject.

Speech Day

The school choir belted out
the words, innocent voices
filling Hackney Town Hall
just across from the Empire
with its music hall turns.

Parents glowed with pride
as the music master smiled
and forgot, briefly,
the River Kwai.

Japan

If I go long-haul again,
I may return to Tokyo
to stare at men in business suits
who wait at zebra crossings
for tweeting birds to sing,
always on time.

If I go long-haul again,
I'd search the pavements
for non-existent litter, sneeze in public,
sometimes spit, as if to prove
that too much courtesy can irk
us Brits (and what about the war?)

If I go long-haul again,
further than that flight from Trinian,
I'll stand by Shima hospital
and wonder how a Little Boy
can vanish eighty thousand souls
into a birdsong sky.

Maths Master I

I am bewitched by symbols
that precisely predict
a particle's slide down rough slopes,
the bounce of balls on perfect tables.

His chalk strokes, sharp
and certain in every detail,
fill my mind with proof
of another life.

Later, we find ourselves
in the same exam room,
trying to unlock futures
with our secret code.

Nothing is said.
We close our books,
exchange no signs,
leave through separate doors.

Examination

On a sloping rectangle of wood
lie objects, instruments
of torture and meditation:

a spike dipped in black blood,
dispensed in fractal curves
over blank sheets;

a flexible block
for erasing all error.

Black cloaks hover
but rarely speak.

A mouth utters words of command
that many do not wish to hear.

The young leave quietly.
Black cloaks remain
to salvage the thin residue
of suffering.

Bogeyman II

He stood behind me
in a bus queue, took me
into A-certificate movies,
left before the Pathé News,
before the lights came on

but I remember him, shouting,
on the screen, shouting,
arm raised, cursing the world
in tongues that tried to touch me,
almost touched me.

My mother told me
to keep my head down.
My mother told me
not to look, but I ran
hard as I could before nightfall.

Making Ghosts

> He smiles, and moves about in ways
> his mother knows, habits of his.
>
> ...
>
> How easy it is to make a ghost.
> > Keith Douglas, *How to Kill*, 1943

1. Wire

July/August 1944

Wires relay mixed messages:
the Führer's dead, alive,
confusions that filter upwards
into the attic, where Anne writes
she's optimistic: *Great News*,
though Stauffenberg's already shot.

Imagine another room:
whitewashed walls, low ceiling,
fixed rail, six meat hooks.
At the side, a small table,
a bottle of cognac and glasses
for the witnesses. The hangman
makes jokes, wears a permanent leer.
In one corner a movie camera;
every detail must be recorded.

The Field Marshall is first.
He makes no sound
as piano wire caresses his neck.
They lift the old soldier, drop him,
pull off his trousers.
He twists in the air.

Typhus takes longer
behind Belsen's barbed wire.

2. Breaking the Rules

23rd January 1945
Erwin Planck, Plötzensee Prison, Berlin

My father didn't want it, this universe
of fragmentation. He didn't even like the atom.
Ultimately it will have to be abandoned
in favour of continuous matter, he insisted.

In his dark suit, starched white shirt
and black bow tie, he looked like a Prussian
civil servant but for the penetrating eyes
under the huge dome of his bald head.

He yearned for the certainties of the past
but the century splintered into relativity,
Schrödinger's Cat, the possibility
of a state between life and death.

We went for a walk in the Grunewald Forest.
I was seven years old and he was full of joy:
Today I have made a discovery
as important as that of Newton

but he hoped the quantum would vanish.

Father, look closely at the world.
The rules have been broken;
there is no going back.

3. Dresden

14th February 1945

See the woman run,
a bundle in her arms;
it traces out an arc
and is consumed,
a child flashing into fire.
A thousand degrees
shrink adults to infants;
the hot wind hurls them
back to burning rooms.
Ash Wednesday: the dying
light their own paths
into darkness.

4. Remagen

March 7th 1945: Ludendorff Bridge

Schiller, Kraft, Strobel, Peters:
tomorrow, the sun will not rise
unless there is more blood.

Why are the gods not appeased?
They brood in silence
as tortured steel refuses to obey.

In Westerwald Forest
traitors rot in shallow graves.
Even a bridge conspires against destiny.

5. Finito

29th April 1945: Milan

How they cheered Il Duce,
a man sent by Providence,
exalted by the Pope himself.
How things change, Clara!

Black shirts melt into shadows
and here, in the Piazzale Loreto,
the glory that was Rome
hangs from a meat hook.

6. Moving Pictures

May 1945: Clock Cinema, Leeds

They search for the stars
through tobacco haze, follow
each washed out image
on the screen. Sweaty-necked
rows of utility suits,
tiredness slumped against
faded seats. Soldiers march
as powdered dolls parade
to music, to victory. Dust
dances in the flicker
of the projector's light.
I want something.
She rummages through her bag,
tells the boy there's nothing left.

Then give me something else.
A killer's eye, perhaps,
or the floating nightmare
of Donovan's Brain, conjuring
bubble spells out of a glass jar,
turning men into monsters.
They shall not pass; Gary Cooper
will meet The End armed
with his righteous gun while Mrs Miniver
survives her clapboard blitz
on the Hollywood back lot.
Now, through cracks in an adult wall
he sees the cock crow its news, hears
the clipped voice as cameras pan

slow as ice across an open pit
of broken extras, jumbled

contortions of skin and bone, stick
origami folded by bulldozers.
In black and white a woman weeps,
men stare, stone-grey
into the winter soil.

There is no hero, no lipstick.
His head is pulled down
into mother's lap. They wait
for the main feature, the
safe return in glorious Technicolor
of the real world,
Ronald Colman to Shangri-La.

7. Lines

June 1945: Berlin-Köpenick

Poland, a moving blood-stain
seeping west from Curzon's line,
congeals as leaders meet and talk

in different tongues, peruse
their well-thumbed maps,
the stab of coloured pins

tattooing grand designs
on Berlin's corpse, laid out
on butchers' slabs.

Red lines incised by scalpels
can't hold back the turbulence
of human flesh in flight

but, for the moment, boots
on bloody ground
are all that count.

The Committee on Dismemberment
of Germany begins its autopsy
while Comrade Molotov suspects

a dirty bourgeois stitch-up.
Never mind, says Uncle Joe,
we'll do it our way

later

8. Trinity

July 16th 1945: New Mexico

Hornig checks
as the needle falls to zero.
Quantum spells, conjured
from the mathematics of men's minds,
flash matter into energy.
No one who saw it could forget
that foul and awesome display.
Bainbridge looks into the heart
of the fireball, grasps
what physics cannot explain,
cameras cannot record:
Now we are all sons of bitches.

*

When Oppenheimer returned to base,
his walk was like High Noon. We'd done it.
My faith in the human mind has been restored, he said
and in the New Mexico dawn Rabi thought of Alfred Nobel,
how dynamite would put an end to war.
                                        Partially eviscerated
wild jack rabbits were found more than eight hundred yards
from Ground Zero where sand fused, translucent as jade,
under the twisted ghost of the metal tower.
Three miles away, farmhouse doors were torn loose
and afterwards Fermi felt unable to drive home.
It seemed to him that the car jumped curve to curve,
skipping the straight stretches of road between.
At 0836 Pacific War Time, four hours after
lightning blanched the face of the moon,
Indianapolis sailed under the Golden Gate.

9. Leaving Okinawa

August 1945: Colonel Yahara

I hear them snigger.
They say I surrendered,
a disgraceful charge
against a *gunjin*.

The plan was *jikyusen* :
Wear down the enemy!
My superiors knew better,
sacrificed a hundred thousand.

The Americans say:
You've done your duty.
When business goes bad,
you start over.

Perhaps, when defeat came
I should have joined my ancestors
but I was never
a prisoner of war.

10. Hiroshima

August 6th 1945

A city unrolls east to west
in the cross hairs of Ferebee's bombsight.
He kills the drift, makes small corrections.
Enola Gay jumps as Little Boy falls away
and Dutch thinks: *I can go home.*
To Lewis, atomic fission tastes like lead
on this fine summer morning
as insects and birds crackle,
vanish, and human beings
transmute into small black bundles
awaiting collection.

11. Operation Paperclip

September 1945: Kransberg Castle

I am an engineer.
My black uniform is neatly pressed
for important meetings.
Himmler appreciated my efforts;
no reason to complain.
We must all work.

I am an engineer.
The moon wants to gather me up,
transport me to another world,
faster than a doodlebug
over London's rubble.

Today, there is a meeting
to decide which side I'm on.
Sturmbannführer
to Herr Professor -
the Americans want me
squeaky clean. It's good
to have friends in high places.

I am only an engineer
but the stars are waiting.

12. Quisling

October 1945: Oslo

Let's face it:
Laval, Mussert, Pavelić, Szálasi
didn't drop from the sky.
They had mothers and fathers,
considered themselves patriots,
defenders of national honour,
even saviours of the race

before they were *traitors*.
There may be reasons, but
we don't want to know them;
it's not the time for analysis,
to dissect childhoods,
the complexity of minds,
the banality of abnormality.

We, the victors, have sentenced them,
these *filthy quislings*, to be hanged
or shot in rain-soaked courtyards
as each family hurries to point a finger
at the monster in its midst, the abuser
who shakes his head in disbelief,
wonders how it's come to this.

13. ENIAC in Nuremberg

November 1945

It's almost finished,
tubes and diodes buzzing,
the flow of sparks
that count the milliseconds,
calculate, predict, enhance
man's terrible potential.

Human to the naked eye,
sit twenty one in rows,
their algorithms run.
Goering, von Ribbentrop,
Streicher and Speer –
they calculated, cast
the dice for sixty million -
so many ones turned to zeroes.

Digital cogs whirr
their coded secrets:
guns and rockets,
A-bombs, H-bombs.
It's all the same,
a blur of numbers
that take no prisoners.

14. United Nations

October to December 1945

And now the cold blood reckoning:
How many litres flowed from unnamed flesh?
How many walls have fallen into dust?
The millions trudge down roads to distant homes,
reclaiming wreckage from the rats, who scurry
in respectable disguises to survive
or smirk at Nuremberg. Lame Europe
moves en masse, while leaders talk,
shake hands and smile, unite
behind new walls, prepare again
for war.

Goons

Bloodnok's war was over,
a pratfall of heroes
fallen in the water,
bluebottles emerging
out of human puree,

uniforms neatly folded.
They came home to roger
Bannister (Minnie, that is)
parped at the world
laughed till they died.

What time is it, Eccles?
No need to write it down.
They spent their days
decoding rhubarb,
the meaning of insanity

à la Spike. He was the last
of them.   His epitaph :
I told you I was ill in Gaelic
although he never spoke it.
This madness is their gift.

Seagoon, Moriarty, Crun,
the well endowed Hugh
Jampton, Grytpype-Thynne.
Where are those manic few?
Deaded, every one.

Maths Master II

Strange to see him across the room,
taking the same degree exam.
He wore that familiar pinstripe suit
as he conjured symbols from the air.

I'm sure his eyes avoided mine
but I caught him as he reached the door.
'Sir, remember me?' *'Of course.
And how are you?'* He feigned surprise.

I bought the teas. We sat a while
facing across the plastic white.
His neat cuff caught the saucer's edge
as we stirred and smiled.

'What comes after your degree?'
he asked me after an awkward pause.
'I'm not sure really. Love the maths,
that's all. And you?'
                    *'I blame the war.
Disrupted life. Just getting back
on track. Perhaps get out of schools,
a college job.'*
                    I gulped my drink.
'Your teaching', I said, 'I must thank you
for that. I think I'll stick with maths.'

His eyes studied the cooling tea,
its depths perturbed by a falling drop.
Together, we watched the wave decay
as we held our breath.

Mathematica Erotica

Still drooling, at my age,
over differential equations,
medication has little effect.
Others shake their heads
as if I have a defect, glaze
at the merest mention of pi,
won't look me in the eye
when I show dissension
about children or nature.
Is that a crime? I mean,
I like a good view, grass,
nameless flowers, but
for a real turn-on
that lasts for hours
give me an integral sign

any time

First Paper

Bullet points steady nerves
as the chairman glowers
and nine inquisitors
half-fill a room,
conference proceedings
cocooned in corduroy laps.

They stare at the thirteen-word title,
something about *stochastic systems*.

He moves forward
to explain everything,
young face glistening
in the projector's light.
His fifteen minutes melt
into a diarrhoea of words,
the black sprawl of equations,
a frantic shuffle of acetate sheets.

A red light flashes; he ignores it.
The world must hear his message.
After twenty minutes
the chairman intervenes;
the conclusion is abrupt.
Time for a question? *Be brief*
then faint applause,
the looks of relief.

Uphill

My father stares at horses in a field
across the road from his son's house.
He can't stop chuckling.
It is the first house I have owned.
My parents are visiting and
no, the flowered wallpaper was not my choice.
I am trying to work in the small kitchen,
wrestling with maths on a Habitat table.
My mother can't possibly stay
in a kitchen without a pinafore
or a proper washing machine
and it's a pity the outside loo doesn't work
and it's a long climb to the bathroom.

She eyes the old spin dryer;
I imagine her wrestling it
across the stone flags
as the truth simmers
in a crumple of A4 sheets.
I grope for another equation,
hope that dad hasn't got lost
on his way up the hill
from the betting shop.
Mother decides to leave her son
to his important work.
She turns her face
to the picture window,
stares down the horses.

Happiness

Three days it takes
at a kitchen table,
sun on my back, face
down into white paper.

Complexity
is reduced to rules,
behaviour rendered
amenable to proof.

The homunculus in my skull
stares at equations, lemmas,
rifles through filing cabinets,
stumbles over symbols.

Martingales may hold the key
but there's a missing step
and logic stretches, strains
to close the gap

as fingers almost touch,
then touch; a spark,
a resolution, soon
the final draft

and on the third day
it is afternoon.
Across the valley
sets a perfect sun

but, in this moment,
happiness is all about
the certainty of
Q.E.D.

Nature

You seem surprised I don't
recognize snowdrops, can't
picture peonies or name
the magnolia in my garden.
I walk for miles inside a skull
dull to such detail.

Behind the house I face the sun
and ignore the weeds, mowing
carpet confusions of moss and grass.
The plum tree is a wreck of branches
hung with the remnants of summer.

My tenderness is lethal, I know.
Forgive this blindness.

Unboiling an Egg

It rattles the pan
as words are spoken.
In heat, he sees sound
drain light from her eyes,
bleach the flush from her skin.

As clarity congeals to white
his guilt can't refold protein,
retract syllables, shock the world
back into primal innocence.
A timer pings in the silence.

Lifeboat

Words are pouring
from his open mouth,
a flood of spittle
washing away plates, cutlery,

the space between them
a heaving sea,
its surface slick
with old resentments.

Her face is a vortex
into which he shouts
his opinions, needs,
politics, philosophy.

She throws out a smile
attempts to deflect
obscure minutiae
that have *ruined his life*.

Her eyes sweep the horizon
for a pea-green boat,
the Marie Celeste,
even the Titanic

as she opens her handbag,
steps into its warm interior,
retrieves a pair of oars
and rows for the nearest exit.

Cold Call

Crisp packets circle the concrete
tundra of platform one, herd
ragged pigeons into a huddle
of feathers beneath my seat.

That look in her eyes, like dead fish
on crushed ice. I belt up my coat.
A gloved hand smears snot drips
that leather to arctic white.

I piss into iceberg porcelain.
The dryer roars from its polar throat
as someone announces cancellation.
My mobile is an igloo brick.

I ring her number.
There's no reply from Antarctica.

Apathy

He was passionate about it,
his obsession twenty four seven,
the answer to the rat race,
he told friends and family,
until they stopped coming.

He gave up everything for it,
didn't go out, refused
to clean the house, himself,
the dog, the cat,
the parakeet.

Merry Christmas!
Who's a pretty boy?
became irrelevant. Philosophy,
politics, words, thoughts
were a no-no.

He slouched in his armchair,
eyes glued to a blank screen.
There was a smell from somewhere
but he couldn't think what it was
so he didn't.

Clock batteries died
along with the days
as the dust piles reached their optimum heights
before collapsing
in a soundless avalanche.

Interesting
he thought.

Tectonics

Only yesterday, we held each other
in an embrace that seemed unbreakable,
rejoiced in the rock of our union.

Beneath our feet, something was changing.
Our vows became molten rivers,
sweeping away all we held true.

The divorce was painful, protracted,
a ripped separation that left Erebus
smouldering in a lifeless freezer

while Darwin headed for the hotspots
of Asia to crash out in slow motion
at the feet of the Himalayas.

These things happen slowly.
Yesterday, we shared everything.
Today, I am a thousand miles away

buried beneath the ice,
while you bask in the sun
on a billion-year cruise.

So Many Prayers

and here's another,
tucked in a crack
in Jerusalem stone,
a scrap of paper
torn from a notebook.

I have scribbled
Peace & Socialism,
not much to ask.
The wall towers above me,
hums to the mumble
of the faithful, waiting
for their Messiah.

I go through the motions, push
my offering between ruined slabs,
place my hands against the rock
and contemplate emptiness.

Above me, an atheist sun
bakes the holy city.
God is out to lunch, leaving
the uniformed young
to laugh and joke,
keeping their weapons close.

Power

Six inches high,
without arms or legs,
Lenin has a constipated look
as if squeezed through a tube
or constrained by force.

A buttoned-down collar jams up
against the neat red beard.
He looks uncomfortable
in his dark frockcoat, green tie
tucked into grey waistcoat.

He is mine for thirteen Euros,
this master of the dialectic,
part of the market he despised,
a commodity for another tourist
revisiting the left dreams of youth.

His bald head is smooth
to the touch, shining
in the store's fluorescent light.
It is like stroking a naked rat
or painted phallus,

a wooden effigy that scares
neither plutocrat nor class traitor.
Nothing lies beneath
the bulging skull
but cheap vodka.

Fair Trade

Cote d'Ivoire 2012

All day he lifts cocoa bags
higher than a grown man,
feels the bike chain cut
into his aching flesh.

In Mali, they promised him a bicycle.
Here he eats corn paste, burnt bananas,
sleeps on a plank, pisses in a can
like the other eighteen.

At night, locked in this tiny room,
only his breath can escape.
Through one small hole, life enters,
more precious than chocolate.

Echoes

Even now, when words burn
like acid in his ear, when
awkward questions choke him
into silence, he imagines her
sitting across the room.
The face is indistinct:
he knows that smile, resigned
to his failings, his inability,
whatever he achieves, to give
meaning to her life. In him
is the man she married, her regrets,
her 'before the war', when the world
was young with dancing.
You'll end up an old maid
was her mother's warning.
Now, she sits
and shakes her head
but the dead
cannot speak
and the voice
at the end
of the line
is not
hers.

Entanglement

There's a ghost that haunts the universe,
a quantum thread that binds our lives
to distant mass, refusing to let go.

Astronomers hold to another truth:
as bodies move apart, attraction fades
and memory weighs nothing out in space.

Shut up and calculate
they tell the homesick astronaut
and yet

I thought I saw you yesterday
and wept.

Parental Care

The last time I heard him laugh
in that way he had, Jack-the-lad
without a thought for tomorrow,
we sat and smiled
while doctors fumbled
with blooded veins
across the narrow aisle.

I can't remember what he said
but his arms did not move
with those workshop rhythms
that I had seen so often,
the skilful thrust
of needle and thimble,
the final snap of thread.

*

In her sheltered flat
she was free to move,
to fall in the night,
clutch at the red cord,
cry on the mat.

In the residential home
she was trapped in her bed,
baked in the heat
of the pissed-in lounge.
Packaged and safe,
in two weeks: dead.

Lost Words

i.m. Allan Muir (1936-2010)

My friend always calls me *mate* when we meet,
prepares toasted cheese on home-baked bread,
talks of philosophy, physics and rhyme
as we walk Welsh rail tracks in the cold.

His bulk slows
                climbing the upward slope
then he stops for breath,
pores over maps as the sunlight fades,
his laughter pounding the path ahead.

We joke the evening glow to dusk.
I say: *You know a lot of maths.*
He shrugs: *There's always more to know.*

                    *

Six foot eight
and hard to miss.
It's rare to roll up at a pub
without provoking
same old

  *What's the weather like
  up there? It must be cold*

and yet he always laughs
as if they've told a classic gag
while real ale gushes down his throat
to lubricate the miles of dust,
the endless chat
                    and now he's lost.
There is no map, no time for beer,
no shelter from October wind
down here
            I feel the cold.

                    *

The world has shrunk to a bed,
window-lit by autumn gloom.
Head held firm, your eyes squint
down the room to where I sit.

Still time for more discussion,
maths or anything of interest,
you push the conversation on
until at last you tire

and the bed is empty;
a mattress turns its back
and no amount of talk
or love can re-ignite
those words,
your fire.

Small Talk

Love is a word I heard at the wake
after his body betrayed him.
Invisible beyond the furnace doors
reduced to his elements
he couldn't respond to the tears,
the guilt of the survivors.

Between the neat rows of canapés
abstractions drifted about,
lost syllables looking for comfort :
loving, forever, good, wonderful
washed down with fruit juice,
beer, prosecco.

Life, that four letter word,
wept on, regardless.

Wilderness

for Sheila

Difficult to get your attention
when you're out in the garden;
so much to do whatever the weather.
Your fingers coax colour out of the earth,
infuse it with longing for distant glens,
the pungent odours of Kenyan safaris.

The garden needs some attention;
I won't tease you for neglecting it
this year. There will be no more
fresh vegetables or rock plants,
no strength to resist the growth
of weeds and decay.

Difficult to get your attention.
It seems to be elsewhere,
your eyes focussed on a point
in the top corner of the room.
Then you look through me
as if I were invisible.

You may have stories to tell
but it's getting late.
You need your sleep
to dream of a garden,
a wildness waiting.

Keyhole

In her dreams
of ovarian cysts
she
    falls

s l o w l y

down
        down
down
        into

an abdomen
insufflated

a dome of carbon
    dioxide

p
  i
     e
        r
           c
              e
                 d

by cannula, trocar,
    fibre optic

pictures,
conversations
between eyes, lips
hidden behind white
    sterility

then
laparoscopic
cholecystectomy,
a small cut

in the soft skin
of her wordless
sleep

Making Sense

I expected an aura of decay
like arum lilies along a canal.
Perhaps it was too soon to tell,
your body still warming the air,
a camellia on your pillow too close.

Next morning, I ate a full English,
reds and yellows dazzling on my plate,
brown vortices staining cracked white,
half-smiles forced in grey offices,
the cool feel of watermarked paper.

Now, I can't recall the aroma
of your skin, the sound of your voice.
There are frozen images, untouched
behind cold glass, the blurred dreams
in which you say nothing intelligible.

Ritual I

As he cried, he noticed a cross on the wall
and almost smiled. Perhaps, she smiled too
at its dumb irrelevance to her passing
as the man from the undertakers ended
the proceedings with familiar incantations
that nobody had requested.

Then the flames, ashes sprinkled
in places she loved: the rose garden, the sea
at Lytham swallowing that dark residue
before we dumped anonymous plastic
in a bin, without ceremony, en route
to afternoon tea by the lake.

Ritual II

Auden was right about suffering,
how it takes place as men in overalls
down all-day breakfasts
and study their phones
while someone weeps at a nearby table.

As usual, the afflicted are left
to stumble through
Yes, I'm bearing up, thank you
and to wake early the day after
and the day after that
with their lists of mundane tasks.

How comforting to start
with a Tesco fry-up,
laughter, a chat about
nothing in particular.

I tick the boxes, keep on talking,
confuse false with true, dreaming
that the moon is cheese,
the earth is flat
and Icarus flew.

Life in the Fast Lane

Twice a week he beats cod
in a pan with a wooden spoon,
shatters its frozen symmetry
until white petals dance
with the packet peas, under
a crust of curried sludge.

This is the closest he comes
to real cooking, an alchemy
of tastes not found in books,
a travesty of past cuisine,
her recipes on scraps of paper
until they disintegrated.

Now, spaghetti and korma
emerge from his freezer,
labels checked for salt and fat.
Now there's a microwave,
a tray, TV news. On cue
life comes in packages and leaves
in bins on Tuesday mornings
black and blue.

Loveless

He left love in an airless locker
and lost the key.
All those youthful fumblings
but he couldn't pick the lock.

Love shouted at the top of her voice.
He heard only the sound
of wind in the hills, the tap-
tapping of chalk on boards

as the locker was moved
to an unfamiliar station,
to Lost Property, where
all the lockers looked the same.

He listens at keyholes
as love whispers in the darkness,
waiting to be redeemed.

Crusoe on Mars

Beneath a double summer moon
I dream of terra, conjure fields
of fertile soil, but when I wake
a precious drip of water measures
days, preserves my bubble thoughts
in sterile plastic, packages of breath.

Red republic? Monarchy of dust?
No matter. Here I'm bound to serve
and rule, my only follower a shadow
gifted by the sun. No footprints here
except my own. No sound except the hiss
of blood's persistent monologue.

Family Room

You don't want to be here
so you roll up this world into a ball,
cocoon it in your husband's lap.
Perhaps you're asleep, exhausted with pleading.
There is little we need to say, relieved
as you stretch out in the sunlight
that beckons through holes
in the screened window.
Perhaps you're listening
as we chat around you.
You look so peaceful,
those worries filed away:
the lists of things to do,
the safety of your children,
the wretched of the earth
who need your clothes,
the persecuted church,
the coming Messiah;
too much reality
even for you.

Obsession

Whatever went wrong that summer
I blame the peacock butterfly.
We lay on the warm grass,
three of us, under a perfect sun.

I whispered *Happy Birthday, Jane*
and the trees nodded their approval
of an immaculate tableau
arranged with consummate care.

Only a god could have sculpted
those cucumber sandwiches,
Fabergé'd each strawberry
to spell out your name.

The butterfly flexed its wings
and a cloud obscured the sun.
I'm not Jane, you said

and walked out of my plan.

Now I could see the trees
were weeping, not nodding,
the cloud darkening overhead.

Jane, if you can hear me:
I have developed a theory
linking chaos to amnesia.

The butterfly is under control now;
its wings move only at my command.
I know I can cure you.

Someone is Home

Switch on :
There's something there.

She meets my gaze,
laughs at my jokes,
caresses my hair.
She's programmed for
Thank you, Please and *Sorry*;
I have ceased to worry
about the uncanny
dispensing care.

So clever these days:
the texture of silicone,
a breath-scent of flowers.
You can't fault the design,
the imperfections
that give peace of mind.

Recharge :
She can talk for hours.

All the words in the world
are in here, somewhere,
a matrix of phrases
delivering cheer.

Switch off
from the subject of death;

she and I disagree.
For her, at least, there is
nothing to fear.

Astronauts

The green, green grass is distant now
and no amount of stretching
compensates for empty space,
as shin bones thin and muscles waste
with needy hearts that ache
for one more g,
that pull of home.

Album

Knossos, Machu Picchu, Troy:
the pages turn, a window open
to a face, eyes shut, a fringe
of brownish hair, then auburn,
who knows where

as years collide
in Bangladesh or Spain,
bleed memories, yearning
to be firm, made flesh.

Southwold, Falmouth, Windermere:
it's sunny on his wedding day.
He counts the images of friends,
still bathed with summer light;

they wait in darkness everywhere,
stare through yellowed cellophane,
impatient for an afterlife.

The multiverse slides through
his upturned hands.
Anything is possible.